REFINED BY FAILURE

BREAKING RULES AND GETTING BURNED

C. LLOYD BROWN

COPPER QUILL

"*This book offers a powerfully authentic and vulnerable illustration of reinvention and discovery that await on the other side of failure. Lloyd's 10 rules are spot on, and deeply rooted in universal principles. They're beautifully articulated and serve as a practical guide to transform not just your business, but also your life.*"

—**Stephen M. R. Covey,** *New York Times* and #1 *Wall Street Journal* bestselling author of *The Speed of Trust*

REFINED BY FAILURE

Breaking Rules and Getting Burned

Copyright © 2021 by C. Lloyd Brown

Paperback: ISBN 978-1-7369221-2-5
Ebook: ISBN 978-1-7369221-0-1

Audiobook available at www.refinedbyfailure.com

Printed in the United States of America

Cataloging-in-Publication Data is on file at the Library of Congress, Washington, DC.

Content Manager/Editors: James Timberlake & April Kelly
Cover Design: Marc Whitaker
Interior Text Design: Sandy Armstrong

Copper Quill Publishing is an imprint of Iron Imprint.
3478 Catclaw Drive, Ste. 237
Abilene, TX 79606

1-325-244-4565
www.ironimprint.com

TABLE OF CONTENTS

FOREWORD

In *Refined by Failure,* Lloyd has written a very compelling and personal story of what happens when you don't follow the rules that you have set up as a leader and CEO. Lloyd's examples are all personal experiences he encountered in his time as a CEO. His stories are extremely candid and personal, opening his heart fully and reflecting on what he did right and what he did wrong. He doesn't hold back in telling where he made his mistakes and experienced failures. More importantly, Lloyd bares his soul about the impact of those decisions on the company, his employees, himself, and his family. This is a gripping, real-life story of what can go wrong when you don't follow your own rules and beliefs.

I have known Lloyd Brown for several years now. First as a CEO-coaching client of mine and, over time, as a personal friend. He is a candid and sincere person who tells it like it is, both when you talk to him and in his writings.

When Lloyd asked me to read the draft and provide input, I was honored to do it. I read the manuscript in one night and couldn't put it down. This book is a fast and compelling read. I personally believe that many of the stories and experiences will resonate with you in both your work and personal life.

This story is gripping, and a little frightening at times, but after reading the entire book, I keep coming back to the idea that if you follow your rules and values, everything will turn out for the best in the end. You need to make sure you learn from your mistakes and keep focused on what you know is right. I'll have this book on my reread list once a year to remind myself what can go wrong if I don't follow my own rules I set out for my business.

Before transitioning into coaching full time, I was a 6-time CEO/President running large, medium, and small international companies with full P&L responsibilities ranging from $2 billion, to $200 million, to $20 million. I've seen a significant number of well-run businesses, as well as those that are struggling.

I've observed, practiced, and experienced many of the ten rules that Lloyd discusses in this book. I've seen these rules successfully followed and also blatantly disregarded in all different sized companies and on several different continents. The insight that Lloyd provides is not just a North American phenomenon, these ten rules exist and should be applied to all types of companies in the Americas, Europe, and Asia.

Remember: failure is an event, it is not who you are. Learn from it and grow.

Best Always,
Michael Marchi

INTRODUCTION

Like many great stories, this book begins at the end.

In June 2020, I was reflecting on my 12 years as the CEO of Smart Chemical. I had just stepped down as part of restructuring the company; due in part to Covid-19, and partly (probably more than I'd like to admit) due to my own failings as a leader.

For several years prior, Steve Brown, a friend and trusted advisor, had been encouraging me to write a book. I decided that this was the day to start.

Originally, I intended to explain how our 10 Rules came to be, how they changed my life, and how young CEOs could apply them to their businesses.

As I began to write this book though, it quickly became obvious that I've learned my lessons the hard way—by breaking my own rules and getting burned!

"But Lloyd," I hear you say, "Aren't rules meant to be broken?"

While that sentiment has become part of our modern culture, the story of Adam and Eve illustrates that there are consequences to breaking rules. Rules are made to provide boundaries in our relationships, our business practices, and our personal lives, and those boundaries ultimately protect us and those most important to us.

Boundaries are like the speed limits, driving lanes, traffic signals, and warning signs that help us get to our destination safely and efficiently. If we go outside those boundaries, we risk hitting hazards that may slow our journey, cause accidents or in the worst cases, stop us from reaching our destination altogether.

This book, because we're beginning with the end, starts with rule number ten: The Learning Rule, and goes in descending order to rule number one: The Trust Rule.

As you'll learn later, you have to give trust to earn trust, so I'll start.

I'll share with you my failures and regrets, and in doing so I'm trusting you to take the lessons that I learned and apply them in your own life. Hopefully your story can be one that ends with fewer burn scars.

Sometimes the truth is ugly, and often embarrassing—especially in my case.

THE LEARNING RULE

We learn from our failures by finding the best way to come back from that failure. We learn from our successes and document them in order to replicate them.

"Are you having an affair?"

Dumbfounded, all I could do was stare back for a moment before replying, "Why would you even say something like that?"

"Lloyd, we've been in Italy for three days and you haven't touched me once."

As her words lingered in my head, a painful realization surfaced . . . *she was right.*

My mind started racing as I realized that truthfully, I *was* having an affair—not with another woman, but with my company. My entire focus, energy, and most importantly, attention had gone to the business in recent months; I was always thinking about it. Even now, lying in bed with my wife, Lora, as we looked out our window at the beautiful Tuscany sunrise, my mind was still on the events of the past six months.

December 10, 2018

This should have been one of the happiest moments of my life, but I felt numb and empty.

I had just closed on the $60-million sale of my company to a private equity group, and that evening there was an impromptu celebration with my—now former—partners. They were whooping it up, because for most of them it was the largest return on investment they'd ever earned. I should have been celebrating with my friends and investors about our spectacular accomplishment, but it all just felt hollow.

The next morning was no improvement when my CFO, Jim, burst into my office. "Lloyd, we're out of money! When the investors closed, they didn't leave us any capital to operate with and we'll need to make a draw on our line of credit. Payroll is due tomorrow."

Shock turned to dismay as I let out a heavy sigh. "OK. Let's get on the phone with the new bank and see if we can get some cash in the account."

Alone–The Problem with Being a "Know It All"

You see, I had re-invested 80 percent of the cash from the sale back into the new partnership. The new partners had emphasized the importance of showing the investors that our management team was committed to the company, and this was especially true for me. To appease them and close the deal, I committed more resources than any of the other managing partners. I'd done this on my own, thinking it was the right decision, without first asking my wife or any other trusted advisors for their input.

Then, there we were, already looking at being out of compliance with our new bank. Named for the mythological, three-headed dog that guards the gates of Hades, our bank was known as the lender of last resort and was notorious for taking control of over-leveraged businesses. In our first conversation with the relationship manager for the bank, it was his understanding that we would not need to draw on our line of credit for several months.

When we were negotiating the sale, we were assured that the business would not be over-leveraged, and that there was plenty of "dry powder" to grow the business. At that moment, I felt defeated. Taking it at face value, I had neglected doing my due diligence. *It felt like I was facing those dogs in hell.*

How was I going to tell my wife that I was going to lose 80 percent of the money from the sale of the company and just as important, what I'd spent the last twelve years building? All the time spent away from both her and my daughter, consumed with the business and nothing to show for it!

How would she respond?

Would she forgive me?

Compounding Stress–Family

On top of all that, I was still dealing with the fallout from moving my mom. The day that we had our celebration for the sale of our business was also the day that I moved my mother from Lubbock, Texas, to a memory care facility in Amarillo that specializes in Alzheimer's. This came on the heels of being awarded guardianship of her, after a prolonged legal battle with her abusive husband.

The journey began when my mom was diagnosed in 2012. Things seemed to be going okay for a few years. Then in May of 2016, at my daughter's graduation celebration, we started seeing signs that my mom was being physically abused. When we saw her that morning, we were shocked by her appearance. She couldn't have weighed more than 90 pounds soaking wet. It was also clear that she wasn't being taken care of properly—she was unclean and very confused. Needless to say that this was emotionally and physically draining for us. My mom had already given me power of attorney over her healthcare and financial decisions. While these provided some protections, it did not provide her physical protection from his neglect, which is what she needed most.

Her husband was sixteen years younger, and his actions made me believe that he was in the relationship for purely self-ish reasons, not because of love. My mom had been through so many tragedies in her life. Losing her own father at only twenty years old, she then lost my dad, the love of her life, at fifty-three. Amazingly, she was awarded a second chance at happiness with my stepdad, only to lose him as well. I'm pretty sure she married this much younger man because she couldn't bear the pain of burying another husband.

In late January 2019, just about two months since moving my mom to Amarillo, the phone rang.

"Your mom has fallen, and we think she's broken something. We're taking her to the hospital. Can you meet her there?"

When I arrived at the hospital, they told me she had broken her hip and she needed surgery. The doctor was quite frank with me. People in my mom's condition don't normally recover from this surgery, but if we do nothing, she would be bedridden for the rest of her life.

Not long after, my wife and I found ourselves singing to my mom in hospice as she peacefully passed away. I'm so grateful that she had made peace with this life and was confident she was going to meet her Lord; because of that, she died very peacefully. I still can't believe she was gone so quickly.

I looked at the clock to mark the time. It was 7:13 a.m. on February 22, 2019. One month to the day from her fall.

Back in Italy

"So . . ." Lora paused to make sure she had my full attention before repeating the question, "are you having an affair?"

At that moment I lost it. Overcome with guilt and shame, I felt like a complete failure. Everything I was feeling came pouring out. All the shame, the feelings of unworthiness and defeat—all of it. Shame is a powerful force and must be dealt with. If you ignore that shame, it will keep you in a world of crazy, doing the same thing over and over again, expecting different results.

I began to realize the compounding effects of my decisions and the effects of my mom's passing as well. It had been a tough road, but I *thought* I'd been pushing through. Thinking I was successfully managing all of these things, I didn't realize how close I was to having a complete breakdown.

Lora was so sweet and understanding, helping me breathe through my panic attack. She reiterated how much she loved me and that together we would make it through this time. Reminding me that we had been through so many struggles, I realized that in time we would see the blessings of that struggle, as we had so many times before. We took the rest of our trip as a time to rest and heal, but I did not stop and ask myself, what, why, and how. While the trip helped me escape the problems and get some much-needed rest, I didn't take the time to learn the lesson that I so desperately needed to learn: *you don't have to do it alone.*

Partners

We had started the company in August of 2008, with only $400,000 in cash and a $600,000 line of credit. My investors and I started as friends; however, partnerships are more difficult than one might think and getting the company to this level of success and ready for a sale had severely damaged our relationships with each other.

One important lesson I learned through all of that is the need to define expectations upfront. As CEO, it is my job to create an environment of clarity, and allowing expectations to remain undefined will always create confusion.

In the past, many times I didn't define clear expectations, because I knew I would be held accountable to those expectations. I was in the habit of making most of my decisions alone, very fast, and without a lot of thought.

This process led to much of the conflict in my relationships; both with my partners, and even at home with my wife and family. Doing it alone leads to doubt, guilt, and shame. It's unhealthy and financially irresponsible to believe that you have all the answers and the wisdom that it takes to run a business, without any input from others.

As I was preparing to write this book, I read *Get Out of Your Own Way* by Dave Hollis. Dave hit me right between the eyes when he started talking about being a "know it all." I spent a lot of my life being a "know it all" and making fast, independent decisions. Then I had to rely on my creativity and problem-solving skills to get myself out of the trouble that the "Know It All Independent Decision Process" inevitably brought.

Andy Andrews, one of my favorite authors, says in his book *The Traveler's Gift*, "God did not give you the discernment to make right decisions all the time. He did, however, grant you the ability to make wrong decisions right."

I have used the quote to validate and justify making quick decisions all by myself. I still believe wholeheartedly in this quote, because CEOs and leaders have to make decisions, and understanding this quote keeps us from analysis paralysis. However, if not careful, it can become an excuse for siloed thinking and rash decisions—the way it did for me.

Many of the challenges I am sharing with you could've been minimized if I had followed these rules:

- Recognize that there is no shame in accepting counsel from those you trust.
- Create clear and defined expectations.
- Most importantly, hold yourself and your team to those expectations.

Hitting the Wall

I can't believe I'm actually still going to purchase this thing.

On Saturday March 28, 2020, I was at a dealership in Oklahoma City waiting to pick up my custom-ordered, brand new, white with red leather interior, 2020 Corvette. When I ordered the car back in September, I expected this to be a fun and exciting day, but it was a very different world back then.

My stress level related to my business was already through the roof at this point, and this was supposed to be a short respite from the unending meetings.

Given the events of the past few months, I'm now feeling extremely guilty for a luxury purchase like this when I'm looking at laying off so many people and closing so many locations. I didn't even know if our company was going to survive.

Earlier in March, Saudi Arabia initiated a price war with Russia, and as a result, American oil prices plummeted from $53 per barrel on February 19, 2020, to a low of negative $41 per barrel by April 20—a $94 drop in just under two months. Compound that with all the economies of the world shutting down for COVID-19, and the future was looking extraordinarily bleak. We'd been having daily calls on how to effectively manage our business and what the long-term future of our company would look like.

As I was waiting to get with the accounting people to pay for the car and drive home, my phone rang; it was the chairman of the board of directors. "Hey Lloyd, do you have a minute?"

Even though the last thing I wanted to do at that moment was have ANOTHER call, I said, "Of course, what's going on?"

He then informed me that the new board of directors had a meeting to which neither I nor Josh, the other founding partner, were invited. The Board had decided in that meeting that the company was too top-heavy, and they'd like for me to step down.

I had barely started to process the words when the happy, smiling salesman came in and interrupted; they were ready for me. We hung up and I sat there trying to hold everything together, but my mind was racing with the ramifications of the call. What was I going to do? Was I going to fight? What would this do to my family? How would Lora respond? Should I even tell her? I feel so alone!

As I got in my new car for my four-hour drive home, I was numb and in shock. At that point, I decided to call my coach, Mike, from CEO Coaching International. Of course, he gave me great advice: I needed to tell Lora. Then he shared that he had been through something similar, that he would help me walk through this, and that eventually it would be okay. After talking to Mike, I called my best friend Kurt, who is also my pastor. He confirmed everything Mike had advised and said that we would make it together. That evening when I got home, Lora had made dinner. I waited until after we ate to tell her the news. In true Lora fashion, she took a moment to gather her thoughts before reassuring me that we would get through this together.

I no longer felt alone!

What's the Point?

We started with Rule 10 to underscore the importance of recognizing the compounding effects that occur when you don't take the learning rule seriously, as we start to review the rest of the 10 rules.

When I was at these transition points, I thought that THIS failure was going to be the one that ended my journey. As a CEO you rely on your intellect, experience, and logic to get you through those moments of fear, and this was no different. Not seeing the failure as a learning opportunity was my mistake. Identifying with your failures doesn't accomplish anything, learning from those failures moves you forward in life.

Viewing your failures as a part of yourself only brings shame, and shame is a very powerful state of mind. Brené Brown does an amazing job of helping define what shame is and what it's not, and learning about shame and the power of it helps you understand how it affects your decisions. This allows you to make more rational decisions when you face these important transition points in your life.

TAKEAWAY

Failure is part of the journey—not the end. Slow down and ask yourself: what do I need to stop, what did I do right and need to repeat, and what do I need to adjust? Learning from both your failures and your successes is how you improve.

THE CELEBRATE RULE

Celebrating business and
personal victories.

Value

It was Kyla's first birthday with our company, and I could see the remnants of tears in her eyes as she came to thank me for the handwritten card. She was so touched that I would take the time to write her a card and thank her for choosing to be on our team, reminding her that she was valued. What she didn't realize was that I did this for all my employees.

Every month during my tenure as CEO, I got a stack of cards for the employees who were celebrating a birthday that month. I took the time to hand write each one, letting them know how special they were to me both as an individual, and as part of our team. When they received those cards, they felt valued because they knew they were worth the time that I took to write them.

The most important thing about celebrating an event like a birthday is that it really connects people. To celebrate, first you must take the time to recognize the individual and get to know them. In doing so, you inevitably become invested in that person and their future.

When creating a culture where you care about each other, you never know how that will impact you personally.

Friendships

As a 17-year-old, I wasn't overly motivated to help others purely out of the kindness of my own heart. However, when a blizzard hit our town, and the Red Cross asked for volunteers with four-wheel-drive, it sounded like the perfect excuse to take my GMC Jimmy on a joy ride through the snow.

As I rolled in, ready to help rescue stranded families and brave the elements, I started to see myself as a bit of a hero. That's when I met Jay, the Volunteer Commander of the local Red Cross. He was in his element; cool under pressure, able to see the whole picture, develop a plan, then calmly and clearly distribute orders to the eager, but inexperienced, volunteers running around the parking lot.

These same qualities would, many years later, make Jay an excellent executive to have in a crisis. After many years of friendship and trust, Jay was my first choice when I needed to bring in a new VP of Environmental Health and Safety. Whenever a crisis hit, it was like being back in that blizzard. Jay was stoic, like the captain of a ship; he stayed focused on getting us through the storm. His orders came quickly, without any excess emotion, until the crisis was over.

This made him an invaluable asset during a crisis, when every second counts.

However, for most businesses the goal is to minimize the number of crises you have to face as an organization. This meant that for the vast majority of any given year, the same characteristics that made him such a great leader in a crisis, made him a difficult leader to work with outside of those circumstances.

I knew this intellectually, but would often find myself defending the tradeoff as worth it, because on the rare occasion we did have issues, I knew I could trust him to handle it.

It wasn't until I started reviewing his team evals that I started to recognize I had a problem.

Employee Evaluations

You add significant complexity to a business when you hire friends and neglect to set boundaries or expectations within those professional and personal relationships. Jay was a guy that you could love and hate at the same time. You loved him because he knew he was passionate about keeping people safe, but sometimes he failed to realize that people needed to be safe *emotionally* with him, as well as physically. The reports were clear, my team was unable to do their best work under Jay's leadership.

His concise and pointed way of speaking became demoralizing over time, as his team never felt they had any wins. Their mistakes were highlighted in a cold, matter-of-fact kind of way, with no attempt to understand the underlying issue or build a path to improvement. My team was suffering under a regime of perfectionism that was never supposed to exist.

The worst part, it was all my fault.

I knew Jay's personality when I hired him, but I never considered what it would be like to work for him. Moreover, when I would hear from others about his leadership style, I would immediately excuse it as, "Jay's Way" and that was the end of the conversation. I let our friendship and my feelings toward him personally, overtake what I knew was best for my company and my team. It was so bad, it wasn't even a secret, the whole company knew Jay was one of my "Sacred Cows" and as a result was untouchable. He knew it too.

> As we go through each chapter of this book, you'll be introduced to a few sacred cows, or "Friends of Lloyd" (FOL), and how those relationships made living up to the ideals of our 10 Rules difficult.

Anytime you start excusing behavior that needs to be called out, you're putting the needs of one person over the needs of the many. In this case it was my needs, not Jay's. My need for him—for who he was to me personally—was prioritized over how he treated others professionally. In retrospect, this cost me significant credibility.

I finally made the difficult decision to confront him about how he treated his department, as I could no longer ignore the fact that he was blatantly ignoring Rule 3, The Golden Rule.

The thing was, I wasn't just firing an employee; I was terminating a friend. Worse, because I had made excuses for so long, he felt like this was coming out of nowhere, taking him by complete surprise. The timing wasn't ideal either, he had just lost his wife a few months before.

He felt betrayed by a friend during a time when he needed one the most.

In the end, my failure forced me to fire a mentor and dear friend—somebody who had been a protector, defender, and advocate for me—all because I didn't address his behaviors soon enough. It wasn't long after, on November 6, a mutual friend called and told me Jay had died, on his 69th birthday.

I had just been on the phone with him two hours earlier wishing him a happy birthday. He was in the bathroom of the DMV at the time, waiting to get his license and said he didn't feel very good. He was so happy to hear from me, nonetheless, and we talked for a few minutes before he said he needed to get back to the lobby, not wanting to miss his turn.

What I learned from our friend, Leonard, was that not long after talking to me, Jay had a massive heart attack and died. I was so sad; I'd lost someone who was always there for me.

Real Connections

That next day, I received a phone call from Christian, a mid-level team member. He was calling to offer his condolences.

Christian knew how much my friendship with Jay meant, because of the connection we made through the handwritten cards and having met him at new employee orientation. There were so many times when I was the recipient of gratitude for writing these birthday cards, and like most times when you do something for others, I ended up getting blessed so much more!

When we were developing our 10 Rules, the Celebrate Rule was included because we wanted to make sure that we acknowledged the contribution and value of our people, and that we memorialized shared experiences. The same is true when it comes to a business.

Applying the Rules

It's important to celebrate growth or change in your business. Then reflect on it and apply The Learning Rule. What failures can we learn from? What successes can we repeat?

That's how you integrate the Learning Rule with the Celebrate Rule. As a bonus, there's usually cake!

Reflecting back on the past twelve-and-a-half years of my life at Smart Chemical, I have to admit that we often neglected to celebrate the business itself. I can't even remember more than a handful of times when we truly stopped and celebrated the numerous business and personal victories that we had in our organization.

We did have consistent small-team celebrations but not corporate celebrations. I now realize it's very important to recognize the business's milestones, and to make a measure of the business, the way you do for a child when they're growing up by marking their growth on the door jam.

Celebrating is important because someday the music will stop, and as in musical chairs, there won't always be a seat left for you.

From 2017 to 2019, our company won the Inc 5000 Fastest-Growing Companies in North America award all three years in a row. It was an exciting time and something truly worth celebrating, as our company was #2075 that first year.

What an achievement! I was so proud.

My business partners and Board weren't impressed.

You see our company was at a transition time and we had gone from a lifestyle business (distributing profits to partners) to an investment platform (building a business to sell). This created a point of conflict as we (the Board and owners) didn't define or understand that the change in business focus meant that growing organically and with acquisitions, like we did, takes lots of cash, and so we brought in Mezzanine financing to fund our growth.

With new financial stakeholders, the company stopped the profit distributions (lifestyle) and except for taxes, put all remaining cash back in the business (investment platform). This lack of understanding led to conflict and ultimately, the decision to hire an investment banking firm in the fall of 2018 to sell the business.

My partners' focus on cash distribution diminished their enthusiasm for our accomplishment, which subdued my own. So, being the know it all that I am, I decided on behalf of my team that they wouldn't want to attend, so I didn't even ask. I didn't even invite my wife to the event!

I ended up attending the INC. 5000 event in Palm Springs, *alone.*

This event was three days with different breakout sessions. There were speakers talking about growing your business, there were networking sessions, and on the final day, there was a massive celebration party honoring all of the companies that made the list.

The event featured several renowned speakers, like Damon John of Shark Tank; Alan Mulally of Ford and Boeing; Brian Smith, founder of UGG boots (whose story really resonated with me); and also Brené Brown, who has since become one of my favorite authors. This event was so inspirational. So many stories of overcoming obstacles, personal tragedy, failure, and hard work.

I kept thinking about who needed to hear this. My team would have taken so much from these speakers, but instead, I was the only one representing our company. Celebrating a truly remarkable achievement with acquaintances and strangers. All of their hard work and sacrifices, and no reward.

Unfortunately, while I always credited the Oil & Gas industry for our growth, I was not giving the credit our team deserved.

Celebrating alone or with strangers is not really celebrating. It makes you feel more alone and isolated. With the lack of enthusiasm of our owners and Board, and no shared experience with the team, we didn't even take the time to attend the 2018 or 2019 events.

What's the Point?

Shared experiences around corporate celebrations fosters real interpersonal connection. Think about the important events in our lives that we share with others: birthdays, graduations, marriages, funerals, holidays. If you're going to have a celebration rule, you have to be intentional by setting specific dates each year to stop and celebrate.

TAKEAWAY

Celebrating recognizes everyone's contributions and value, and builds lasting memories that lead to strong relationships.

THE COMMITMENT RULE

"One million dollars!"

I was hoping I'd heard him wrong.

"The forecast wasn't accurate." The panic emanating from my CFO was palpable. "I didn't account for all the franchise taxes we'll have to pay."

I knew what he was going to say next before the words left his mouth.

"Lloyd, we're not going to be able to make our numbers."

The words hit me like a punch to the gut. Only the month before, I'd promised our partners a large equity distribution, and negotiated bonuses for myself and the team. The board had already approved and paid out that money in good faith, based on the last financial report from our CFO.

My credibility with the board was already in question based on the underperformance of the Mid-Continent Group, and this was just one more straw on the camel's already strained back.

The Real Deal with Commitment

Definition, **Commitment:** *the state of being dedicated to a cause or activity; a pledge.*

Of all the rules, I believe that the Commitment Rule is really key to building a culture of success.

I think about the many times in my organization, and in my personal life, that I made or received a commitment and believed that we had an agreement. Unfortunately, I rarely took the time or effort to define what we were committing to. I didn't define the time frame or the consequences of success—or failure.

A commitment must be defined and understood by both individuals. Which means that you, as the CEO, need to define clear expectations before asking for a commitment or giving a commitment. Defining expectations for success and also for corrective action if we miss the mark is an integral part of every commitment, big or small.

The 3 Commitments

As a CEO, these are the three most common types of commitments you will need to define and prioritize:

- Process
- Vision
- Heart

Process Commitment

"Children have never been very good at listening to their elders, but they have never failed to imitate them."
—James Baldwin

"Did you get your oil changed like you said you would?"

"Not yet. I'll try to do it today." My daughter Bailey was busy packing her lunch for school as I had my coffee and croissants.

Putting on my best Yoda voice, I turned my croissants into ears, looked her dead in the eye, and said: "Do or do not. There is no try!"

Rolling her eyes while laughing, she said, "Daaaaad, I get it."

"Bailey, I know you get frustrated about this, and having to get your oil changed, but this is important, and I need your commitment that you'll do it regularly. How can you expect to rely on your car if it can't rely on you? When you say you'll 'try' instead of 'I'll do it' that just gives you an easy out when you don't want to do it."

"Ok, I'll stop saying 'try.' But in return you have to promise me one thing."

Still channeling Yoda, I replied, "Powerful you have become, the dark side I sense in you."

"Nope! Stop right there, you can never, ever do your terrible Yoda impression again. Deal?"

"Ok. I'll 'try.'"

A process commitment involves agreeing to complete a task. A simple checkmark. It's either done, or not. This is the most common—and most broken—type of commitment.

The words "try" and "maybe" have become something people commonly use so they can have an "out" when being asked to make a decision or a commitment. When you're the CEO, people want to say yes to you. When they can't say yes, but are not comfortable saying no, they default to "I'll give it my best shot," or "I'll try," in order to try to placate you in the moment and figure out a solution later.

Too often we don't slow down and commit the time that is needed to understand what we are promising to do. The parties or individuals must define the consequences of not keeping the commitment.

Having a strong process for this is essential. *Defining* the commitment is the beginning of the commitment rule. It means that the organization, and you as its leader, have invested the time to think about and develop a process that is clear and repeatable.

Process-oriented commitments usually take very little time for clarification, yes or no should be the standard for this type of commitment. Examples are: picking up a package, changing the oil on a vehicle, calling someone, and other things we commit to routinely.

Commit to train your team to do this, and communicate the importance of the process. Clearly defining expectations at the beginning will make future decisions easier, while planting the seed for the Vision Commitment.

Vision Commitment

In 2015, we started an expansion into the district called "The Mid-Continent."

The name came from a defined area of the Texas Panhandle, Oklahoma, and Kansas and was used by many in the Oil & Gas industry.

I hired a very dynamic manager; he had great customer relationships and had an eye for talent. This manager had a one year non-compete with his former employer. He used the time to recruit new team members and solicit business with companies his non-compete did not cover.

We built a business plan for the expansion and started onboarding new team members, in accordance with our projected forecast. However, the new business did not come on as quickly as promised. Instead of holding him to his commitment and making adjustments, I accepted his excuses and instead provided additional resources to cover the increasing costs.

After the first full year, the operation lost close to **$500,000**.

The board and other team members asked valid and important questions, but I repeated his excuses and protected the manager. All the while reaffirming the original commitment. I justified my decision because we had several highly profitable operations providing enough cashflow that I could divert their profits to offset the mounting losses.

The Mid-Con area continued to lose money for three years.

The Vision I gave to the Board, the investors, and senior leadership did not include a plan to make changes if the expansion plan was not successful. My failure to develop this process also failed my direct reports, since they had no processes to use with their own teams.

We should have reinvested resources in the successful operations to preserve the value created, and focused on reducing or eliminating the operations that were underperforming. This high-level failure made it impossible for my team leaders to execute the plan successfully, because there was no plan to execute. I mistakenly thought that we could just figure it out as we went.

Vision commitments have longer time frames, more personnel, and more financial resources, and should therefore take more time to understand and define. "Due by" dates or evaluation dates for Vision Commitments are mandatory. Examples are budgets, construction projects, employee development plans, and maintenance contracts.

Conflict with my board, my investors, and my team increased because there was no detailed plan if the expansion failed. Vision commitments must involve plans for how you are going to deal with the challenges that arise in business, both good and bad.

This next level of commitment is what separates a manager from a leader: the Heart Level.

Heart Commitment

Heart commitment is the hardest, and the most important. This commitment level requires a leader to "dare greatly." In Brené Brown's book, *Daring Greatly*, she talks about being vulnerable and understanding that you're all in and fully engaged when you take that courageous step into a Heart Level commitment. She uses the speech by Teddy Roosevelt, "Citizenship in a Republic," sometimes referred to as the "Man in the Arena" speech. The heart decision is really a lifelong decision and doesn't have an end date.

"It is not the critic who counts; not the man who points out how the strong man stumbles, or where the doer of deeds could have done them better.

The credit belongs to the man who is actually in the arena, whose face is marred by dust and sweat and blood; who strives valiantly; who errs, who comes short again and again, because there is no effort without error and shortcoming; but who does actually strive to do the deeds; who knows great enthusiasms, the great devotions;

. . . who spends himself in a worthy cause; who at the best knows in the end the triumph of high achievement, and who at the worst, if he fails, at least fails while daring greatly, so that his place shall never be with those cold and timid souls who neither know victory nor defeat."

—Teddy Roosevelt

Defining expectations and holding others accountable, while building a culture of trust within your team, requires something I like to call "Passionate Honesty."

———————

"I'm done!" Lora said to me as I walked in from fishing with a friend.

I looked at her, dumbfounded, and said, "Good to see you too!"

She said, "I'm serious, I'm done. Did you even read the book?"

She was talking about Dave Hollis's book, *Get Out of Your Own Way*. "Yes, I did on the way up there and back."

"Well, I'm done Lloyd. I'm done doing things your way, no communication, following you blindly, expecting you to change. I'm not living like this anymore."

You see, I had made many promises to change over the years, but the changes never lasted. My true desire was to change, but without understanding "why" I made decisions the way I did, there was no way to change.

We both had just finished reading Dave's book. This book led us both to "Heart Decisions." For Lora, her decision was to get off the "Crazy Train" of living with me always on the edge of destruction, only learning about problems when I was in crisis.

For me, I decided that first I would admit that I was a "Know It All." Second, I would work on my mind–as Dave said in his book, "Working out a muscle in your arm doesn't imply you had bad arms before they were strong, but for some reason digging into why we do the things we do, how we're motivated, our habits, what we focus on—that work seems to call into question something at our core that defines us as either strong or weak, fit for more or destined for less, born with it or not."

Back in 2015, I had decided to get physically healthy. I engaged an age management doctor, Patrick, who has a program that sets your base line to where you are physically, and then develops a plan to get you back to a healthy place. When I started the program, I was 233 pounds, 36% body fat, and pre-diabetic. He has a DEXA Scanner by Lunar Prodigy, a machine that scans your bone, muscle, and fat. This machine then gives you a picture of your whole body in great detail, and you can see where your muscle and fat are located.

I call this machine the "truth teller," because when you look at your picture, you can't lie to yourself that you're still in pretty good shape. Over the past six years, that decision has been incredibly beneficial to me and has changed how I look at food and what real physical health is.

Dave's statement made me realize I had left out the most important, most powerful physical attribute—my mind. It was time to start working on becoming truly healthy, spirit, body, *and mind.*

I looked at Lora. "I understand what you're saying and I agree. I'm going to get help." That moment I contacted a therapist for an appointment.

Being brutally honest about your expectations and how the other person is meeting them (or not) is essential to any manager's toolkit. However, leaders temper this with empathy and true care for the individual. This kind of honesty only works because it's coming from a place of true passion not just for the business, but for their wellbeing. That's where the heart level commitment comes in.

Lora was brutally honest!

This type of honesty does not always come naturally to people.

───────── ⌣ ─────────

"I feel like such a hard ass sometimes." Danny was looking at me earnestly; he was a kind man and worried that his hardline stance on commitments with the service companies he worked with was too harsh.

"Why would you say that you're being a hard ass when all you're doing is keeping someone accountable for commitments that they've made, and those commitments are in writing?"

"That's a good question. I hadn't thought about it that way."

"It seems to me like you're being a good leader by having clear expectations and holding your people accountable to the commitments they make."

In today's society, it seems to be so unusual for people and companies to keep their actual commitments, that when somebody holds others accountable to their commitments, they are a "hard ass" or mean. When in reality, holding someone to their commitments is one of the kindest things you can do.

Danny saw himself as being blunt or callous. I and others, however, perceived him as being honest and direct. We always knew that he would do what he said, and that he'd make sure we did what we said. Something he saw as a weakness was one of the things I respected most about him. Danny has been my longest customer relationship and from the very beginning, he defined his expectations: commitment to transparency, always being above reproach, and keeping your word. My respect for him is unmatched and I'm proud to have him as a friend!

What's the Point?

Good or bad relationships are defined and measured by whether or not we made, defined, and kept our commitments. I now know that all CEOs are evaluated by this measure. When you make a commitment, you're saying that you will put forth your best effort and that you will follow through on your commitment. You plan for success, create contingencies for failure, and establish timelines for everyone involved to review the plan and how they'll keep their commitment.

TAKEAWAY
Defining commitment is about clarity, and clarity builds and protects relationships.

THE ZIG RULE

Help others get what they want and
eventually you will get what you want.

Growing up as the son of Cecil Brown—Christian, business
owner, civic leader, philanthropist, and my hero—was a blessing in many obvious ways, but also a curse. The curse was that I
believed I was better than other people because of his success and
stature. On July 16, 1984, he was killed in a car accident. My hero,
and the man whose persona greatly influenced my own, was gone.
I was only 20 years old.

About nine years later, in March 1993, I had to come to grips
with the fact that I was responsible for my own decisions to define
who I was going to be.

Driving 65 miles an hour going east on I40, heading home
to Amarillo, I reached over to the passenger floorboard to pick
up a map. As I did so, I went onto the shoulder and sideswiped

a pickup. Had I been even a few inches to the left I would have missed the truck, and if I'd been 12 inches to the right, it would have been a direct hit.

This accident brought something into clear focus for me: life is precious. I realized that I hadn't been treating others as unique individuals worthy of respect. My ongoing marital problems and interpersonal issues prompted me to evaluate what kind of person I was going to be. Would I continue to be an ego-driven, assumptive-persona, angry, abusive husband and employee? Or would I follow the example my dad set, and become the servant leader that Jesus exemplified?

I chose the latter.

While I was unable to save my marriage, through counseling I was able to release the anger I felt from losing my dad. During this time, I was promoted from senior account manager to district manager at BJ Unichem. In February of 1994, I met Lora, and we married on May 6, 1995. Our daughter Bailey joined us in 1998. I was blessed with professional growth—my district grew from four employees when I was promoted, to 23 direct reports in 1998. It was during this time that I decided to grow into the great leader I had resolved to be, both at work and at home. I just didn't know how.

The Secret to Real Success

"Nobody cares how much you know,
until they know how much you care."
—Teddy Roosevelt

There were about fifteen of us sitting around the breakfast table, almost unable to believe where we were at that moment, and who we were with. We'd paid to have breakfast with celebrated author and my personal hero, Mr. Zig Ziglar.

Zig, as he insisted on being called, was so humble, affable, attentive, and caring. Of course he shared his stories of success, but what impressed me most was that he shared his failures as well.

At the end of breakfast, Zig provided a Q&A session for all of us. When it came my turn, I asked him a question similar to the scene from *City Slickers*, when Billy Crystal asks, "what's the secret to life?"

"Zig," I said, "of all of your lessons, if it came down to one rule, what would it be?"

He said, "Help others get what they want and eventually you'll get everything you want."

That simple lesson from Zig resonated with me.

It changed me, and it changed my thoughts on how to lead a team. It was at this time I realized that people didn't work *for* me but *with* me. I started introducing my team not as my employees, but as people I worked with. Everyone has a choice of what company they work for, which meant they made a deliberate choice to work with me. I decided that I wanted to be worthy of that choice, and strived to earn their respect daily.

I believe with all my heart that this mindset has been the foundation of the business success I've experienced.

Stephen Covey Influence–Foundation

"Seek to Understand, then to be Understood."
—Stephen R. Covey

If Zig's rule is the "what," then Stephen R. Covey taught me the "how."

While working with BJ Unichem, they sent us to a weeklong corporate training using his book, *The Seven Habits of Highly Successful People*, as the foundation for the culture of BJ Services.

"Seek to understand, then to be understood," is the foundation of learning what your customer wants. In order to seek to understand, you have to get really good at asking questions and become an active listener, which is the "how."

Nurturing the Roots of Business

A tree will grow fast and become strong when it has healthy roots that grow deep and wide. Just like a tree, your business will grow, but only if it is planted in fertile soil.

For a business, your three primary roots are the stakeholders: customers, employees, and equity partners. If you neglect any of these, your company will not grow to its full potential, and you will invite conflict and strife within your organization.

Customers–Building A Better Well

Our relationship with Terry began when we showed his company our amazing laboratory results, and sold them on the benefit to their gas wells. Our program was more expensive; however, the lab results and initial well tests showed real value. Based on the limited amount of data, it appeared our chemical program would pay for itself in less than two months. When you sell a benefit, you must always determine what success looks like and how you will measure that success. That will always come down to money.

During a downturn in commodity prices, Terry was laid off, as he was one of the most highly compensated employees at the company. Terry's former boss also decided that they would forgo using our product, after two solid years of exclusivity. Unfortunately, we had not followed through with consistently showing the value of our program and the return on investment. We had relied on Terry's knowledge and understanding of our value and when he was gone, we had nothing but old evidence to stand on. They started using a commodity product that was much less expensive and was sold as a substitute for our product. Three years later, Terry's replacement called us back saying they had done a study on well performance. Our wells had significantly outperformed the commodity solutions wells when comparing the last three years versus the years we had the business (which did not surprise us).

We were asked to come back and resell our program. This time we focused on how our customer was going to measure performance going forward, and how we could best serve them. Before we lost their business, we had become overconfident and took the relationship for granted. However, when given the chance to begin again, we became much more customer oriented and focused on being easy to work with, providing a total package. We made sure to outline how success was going to be determined and monitored.

Employees

Alex, a member of my team at BJ Unichem, injured his back while on the job and was sent to a surgeon for a ruptured disc. The spinal fusion surgery was going to cost about $80,000, and Alex would have a 25-pound lifting limit for the rest of his life. He would have to either change jobs in our organization, or leave the organization and find a new line of work entirely.

I had learned about an experimental option to repair the disc using a spinal tap and a laser. However, this minimally invasive procedure was not an approved treatment for this type of injury by our workers compensation insurance, and required a special waiver by our insurance carrier and the Vice President of Human Resources.

I met with HR to advocate for Alex, who was in his late 20s at the time, to have the option of attempting this experimental treatment—which only cost a tenth of the approved surgery. The VP said yes and to our relief, the surgery was successful. Alex eventually left BJ Unichem and continued to find success in the oil and gas industry.

In 2017, I got a call from my founding partner, Josh. He said, "You're never gonna believe who is at my house . . . Alex Sampson! He's here managing a job I'm having done at my home."

I learned that Alex had a successful amateur bodybuilding career, that he was an avid mountain bike rider, and had been living a very dynamic life. As we became reacquainted, I was amazed at the management skills that Alex had developed since leaving BJ Unichem.

Coincidentally, we had a need for someone with his skills, and he agreed to come to work for Smart Chemical in a field management role. He rose quickly into senior management and was an amazing team leader.

My goal at the time of Alex's surgery had been simply to help an employee get the treatment that would be best for his long-term success. I had no idea that, 20 years later, that same employee would become an outstanding leader in my own company.

Equity Partners–Building Smart Chemical

Equity partners are often the first people that say yes to your vision. In the case of Smart Chemical, it was my founding partners, Josh and Stephen, as well as our first investors. Initially, understanding what your equity partners want is pretty simple. They want the business plan to be executed to provide the value and return on investment you've promised.

We started Smart Chemical August 1, 2008. The price of oil was $125 per barrel and natural gas was $10 per million British thermal units (MMBtu). Our business plan and the profits generated by that plan looked incredible. In our first month, we did over $200,000 of business and our second month was very close to that.

Every one of the equity partners and I were high fiving each other for our incredible start.

"Everyone has a plan 'till they get punched in the mouth."
–Mike Tyson

However, business plans are only good on the day that they are published. A business is dynamic and has so many different forces influencing the decisions that must be made for its success.

———————— ᶽ ————————

"Is this as bad as it seems?"

It was September 15, 2008, and I was in Banff, Canada, at a risk management conference with some of the largest businesses in the insurance industry. I was having a conversation with one of the risk managers from AIG, the largest insurance carrier in the world at the time, as the announcement that the Lehman brothers had just filed for bankruptcy spread through the conference.

"It could be really bad," he said, grimly.

By January, the price of oil had dropped to around $30 a barrel, with natural gas at $3/MMBtu, in what we now know was the beginning of what would become the 2009 financial crisis.

Crisis

"We're all either in crisis, coming out of crisis or heading into a crisis."
—Andy Andrews, *The Noticer*

Our revenue dropped by 90 percent, essentially overnight.

We did what any young company would do in that situation: we went from eight employees down to four. I took no salary, and the other two founding partners took half salaries, one even taking a part time job for another chemical company as a consultant just to make ends meet.

By September 2009, our company was $1 million in the red, most of which we owed to our main manufacturing partner, Magnablend. The investment partners made it clear they would not front any more money. To save the company, two other partners and I took out personal IOUs to maintain the relationship with Magnablend owners Dave and Scott Pendry. Their willingness to work with us was a testament to our relationship, as well as their belief in us and Smart Chemical.

One thing that's clear about the oil and gas industry is that business can change extremely fast. In the last quarter of 2009, we landed a new customer, EXCO, which allowed us to recoup our losses enough to begin 2010 in the black and bring on three new equity partners shortly after.

By the end of 2011, we had paid off all of our debt, repaid our financial partners 250 percent of their original investment, and gained 50 percent equity for me, Josh, and Stephen combined.

What's the Point?

There is a universal law that when you give, you always receive much more.

Dave and Scott's trust and gift of credit was returned to them 10X over the next two years.

Our equity partners' initial investment of $1 million of cash and loan guarantees netted them a return of over 30X in cash flow and proceeds from the sale of the business.

Personally and professionally, helping Alex get the medical care he needed has paid dividends to this day, and he has become an incredible leader in the company.

TAKEAWAY

The key to serving and leading is helping others get what they want without the expectation of getting something back. That being said, usually you receive more than you give.

THE BEST RULE

Defining "The Best"

I was looking in the mirror and asking myself what I could have done better.

It was Sunday morning March 29, 2020. The afternoon before, I was asked by my board of directors to step down as CEO. The company needed to get lean to survive, they said.

I kept telling myself I had done my best, but looking in the mirror, I knew that I had not.

"The Best" is based on your own personal **mark**, or goal. As every individual is unique, so "The Best" is individual and unique.

A CEO's job is recognizing the attributes, skills, and talents required to do a job, providing a minimum expectation to fulfill that role. However, the expectation is that the Mark for an employee will change over time as they perform the job.

> **Mark**–A defined ability that is calculated by multiplying your God-given talents, the investment in you by family/friends, educators, mentors, and self. Your Mark is unique to you and therefore the Mark is different for every person. The Mark should be ever-changing until the day you die. When we understand that each of us is totally unique, comparing ourselves to others is destructive. The best for one person is an individual measurement and can only be truly measured by our creator.

When you go to the doctor's office, they don't compare you to their other patients, but rather yourself. They review your stats in relation to the last time they examined you, and compare your test results, measurements, and symptoms to look for areas of improvement and areas of concern. If you are on medication and not improving, they may adjust your levels or they may ask you to change your diet, depending on your unique situation.

In a similar way, leaders need to compare team members with their past selves, not other team members. While the team's average performance may give you a standard to use as a benchmark, tracking the actual improvement, or lack thereof, of an individual requires direct contrasting with the team member's past performance. If there is no improvement, that is a red flag; either a lack of training, or their engagement is the issue. Either way, you can address the specific issue and facilitate growth. The old saying, *if you're not growing, you're dying,* is true here.

The CEO's job is to set the expectations for how the company's Mark is going to be implemented for it to be its Best. Defining the expectations for frequency of training and measuring progress through evaluations are critical to a culture that strives for "The Best." The CEO has to implement and model the definition of the Mark with his direct reports. Then this should be replicated by operating groups throughout the organization. Expecting the Best without structure and high expectations will result in disappointment and turnover. Without structure and high expectations, you will get what you deserve, not what you want. The old adage, *you can't manage what you don't measure* applies to the Mark.

Attitude

But having the resources and skills is not enough. Effectively using the time invested requires each of us to make a decision about our mental state or better yet, our attitude. A positive attitude is the decision that is the foundation of the Best Rule. The definition of attitude is a settled way of thinking or feeling about someone or something, typically one that is reflected in a person's behavior. Positive, as defined for this discussion, is an attitude that is constructive, optimistic, and confident. Traits associated with a positive attitude are openness, helpfulness, happiness, encouraging, coachable, etc.

We use our time best when we have these positive traits. In all my years of management, I've never offboarded a team member that had a positive attitude. I have reassigned team members, and I've helped them find a career somewhere else when needed—a place where they were hired into a role where their skills, gifts, and talents were the best fit for that organization. However, in almost every case where I've actually had to offboard a team member, their attitude was always a contributing factor. Your Best can never be accomplished with a negative attitude.

It was January 2019, our second month with new partners, and my CFO had just finished our financials for December 2018. Jim came in and announced we had lost $800,000 in the month of December. Now I was preparing for our board meeting, trying to figure out how to explain how we did not see this coming. Thinking back to April 2018, I remembered that a trusted advisor had warned me as we entered into our process to sell the business that I needed be aware of the time, effort, and energy needed to market and represent the business—that it would be very vulnerable to running off track and losing its momentum.

I was so arrogant that when he told me that, I immediately thought, "Not me, not my team. We're running really well and things are going smooth, we're great!"

We *were* having record months and gaining new customers. Things really couldn't have been better. What I didn't realize was that the way we managed the business would change due to the marketing and sale of the business (just as my friend had advised). Now, we were focused on making our monthly numbers because the investment banking team was focused on the monthly projections in the marketing plan. They communicated that every little change was going to be scrutinized by the companies that were interested in investing in our company. This changes how you run the business.

That was when we quit focusing on the future. We were no longer looking down the highway for opportunities and threats, but rather simply looking at what was directly in front of us, week to week, month to month. We started missing the warning signs. *I* started missing the warning signs. Jim, our CFO and a very good friend, was heavily involved in the marketing and sale efforts as well as focusing on hitting the numbers. We had numerous presentations and dinners—doing everything that it took to market the business.

Looking back, warning signs indicating volatility were visible but we were so focused on the sale we missed them. Running the company to hit the near-term goals blinded us to what many people in our industry saw, as well as our internal indicators, which predicted a slowdown. My arrogance kept me from being my best, and it kept me from recognizing that if Jim and I were going to be focusing on the sale process of the business, we needed to empower some of our great team and challenge them to be the ones looking out into the future to make sure that we weren't heading for trouble.

Arrogance is a bad attitude! A CEO will never be their best with an arrogant attitude. It is impossible to be your best if you are arrogant, and being a know it all is the pinnacle of arrogance. In hindsight, it really was the best that I could do at the time, because I didn't realize I had blinders on. Not being self-aware really limited what my Mark—and therefore my Best—could be at that time. So we missed the upcoming downturn.

Competency

The next step is nature's law of repetition. This law states that repetition creates competency. Noel Birch introduced a learning model in the 1970s as an employee of the Gordon Training International called the 4 States of Competence. The four states are: Unconscious Incompetence, Conscious Incompetence, Conscious Competence, and Unconscious Competence.

For everyone born on this earth, for everything that we do in life, there is a first time. The first time we do a task is usually the slowest. The first time we do something is an adventure. It can also be scary, exhilarating, painful, and confidence building. Riding a bike is a great example of a first-time scary experience. But as we do it more and more, it becomes easy and can almost be done unconsciously. So, to be our best and to do our best requires repetition. Training is also part of that competency.

You are unaware of the skill and you lack proficiency	*You are aware of the skill but are not yet proficient*	*You are able to use the skill but only with effort*	*Performing the skill becomes automatic*

Sir Richard Branson said, "Train people well enough so they can leave, treat them well enough so they will stay." I always wanted to have an organization that promoted from within. However, that can't be done without training people not only in their current job, but training them to promote as well. I have a friend, Shawn Twing, who is a Labor and Employment Law attorney. He has also represented our company on several occasions. Recently we had a conversation about promoting from within. He does training and consulting for companies as part of his legal practice.

He told me that in his training he asks the attendees, "Please raise your hand if you were promoted from within into your management position." The overwhelming majority raise their hand. He then asks them to keep it raised if they received any management training prior to taking the job, and over 90 percent lower their hand. As Laurence J. Peter defined in his Peter Principle: employees are promoted based on their success in previous jobs until they reach a level at which they are no longer competent, as skills in one job do not necessarily translate to another. Another way of saying this is, *we take someone who is unconsciously* competent in their current job and promote them into one where *they are unconsciously incompetent.* To promote from within, a company's training program must make sure that the employee is, at a minimum, performing their job by being consciously competent with the ability to become unconsciously competent.

Awareness

Definition, **Awareness:** *knowledge or perception of a situation or fact.*

Not being self-aware limits what our best can be.

I became "Aware" by starting the process of self-examination when I was looking in the mirror. I came to realize that making a compromise, taking a shortcut, or ignoring problems altogether thinking, "I'll take care of it later," or worse yet, "I'm a great problem solver and I'll always have time to fix it," is not good leadership.

As I looked in the mirror on that Sunday morning, I realized that there was not gonna be any more time to fix it. You see I had been really good at always getting myself out of trouble. I had viewed my problem-solving skills as a way of making decisions without enough information, just on my gut feelings, and if they didn't work out, I could always fix them.

In chapter one, we talked about the Andy Andrews quote, "God did not give you the discernment to make right decisions all the time. He did, however, grant you the ability to make wrong decisions right," and how I used this quote to defend making fast decisions and using my problem-solving skills, and I now realized that I had missed Andy's real message for all these years. I was just fixing the consequences of the wrong decision, not making it right. Solving the consequences of bad decisions is not making them right; it's like treating the symptoms of a disease, not the disease itself. You feel better, but you're still sick.

Well, COVID-19 and the war on American oil by Saudi Arabia and Russia killed me in my role as CEO. My death certificate as the CEO of Smart should read, COVID-19/Saudi Arabia/Russia, co-morbidity, Arrogance.

Looking at Myself in the Mirror

As I've gotten older, I've made a practice of going to the dermatologist.

There are times I'll ask him about a spot and he'll look at it and say it's nothing to worry about, but there are many times he'll notice something I completely missed. Because I look at myself every day, I don't notice the small changes. During my annual visits, however, those changes, taken in aggregate when seen by my doctor, are very noticeable.

The role of the CEO is to examine the business.

Just like the dermatologist, you must look for areas to improve and also for potential worrying signs that often go unnoticed day to day. This involves looking for imperfections, areas that need correction or improvement, or things that may need to be removed altogether.

Just like you need to hold the mirror for members of your team, it's very important that you find someone to hold the mirror up for you. This needs to be someone who does not have a direct investment in your company. When someone has a financial investment in your company, they have a very difficult time being unbiased.

My solution was to join a group called Vistage, a group of peer CEOs that meet with a facilitator. The group practices holding the mirror for one another, asking the hard questions and processing challenges. Vistage provides world-class speakers on many subjects focusing on best practices and solutions for businesses.

These speakers hold mirrors that find flaws in specific areas of your business and then provide tools to improve.

Time

Procrastination is a disease that, like cancer, consumes a person and a company's most valuable resource: time.

When we are born, the date and time are on our birth certificate. Therefore, we need to think of time as a bank account. The day we are born, time begins to be withdrawn from your account by 1,440 minutes every day, and 525,000 every year. You can never put time back into your account, once gone it is gone forever. When we die, on our death certificate is the date and time; this indicates that your account is empty.

The Best Rule relates to the understanding that we exchange our most valuable and diminishing resource, *time*, for work, play, relationships, education and so on. This is why during our younger years, the values and education that are invested in us are so very important. It provides us the resources and skills to make the most out of the years when we start working. I believe that we should teach all students about the true cost of not focusing on the best use of our most precious and diminishing resource. I call this invested time, Rate of Return. Managing time is really a misnomer, as how do you manage something that you have no control over? Our time clock cannot be stopped. However, we can choose where we spend our time. Every human needs to understand that where, or on what, they spend their time is a trade for that something. Time can be exchanged for work, money, education, practicing, mental fitness, physical fitness, relationships, escape, and the list can go on and on.

THE DASH

I read of a man who stood to speak at the funeral
of a friend. He referred to the dates on the
tombstone from the beginning… to the end.

He noted that first came the date of birth and spoke of
the following date with tears, but he said what mattered
most of all was the dash between those years.

For that dash represents all the time they spent
alive on earth and now only those who loved
them know what that little line is worth.

For it matters not, how much we own, the
cars … the house … the cash. What matters is how
we live and love and how we spend our dash.

So think about this long and hard; are there things
you'd like to change? For you never know how
much time is left that still can be rearranged.

To be less quick to anger and show appreciation more and
love the people in our lives like we've never loved before.

If we treat each other with respect and more
often wear a smile… remembering that this
special dash might only last a little while.

So when your eulogy is being read, with your life's
actions to rehash, would you be proud of the things
they say about how you lived your dash?

What's the Point?

Striving for our individual and collective Bests keeps the team and organization healthy. The Best is not a standard, but an aspirational milestone unique to every individual and every company. It is ever-changing, based on where we are in our life cycle. Our physical, mental, and life experiences are always changing every day from the moment we are born until we die.

TAKEAWAY

CEOs must have a sense of urgency and be dedicated to defining the best for the organization and each individual team member.

THE VIGOROUS DEBATE RULE

Jim was obviously very uncomfortable. "What's up Jim?" I said, trying to draw him out.

"Have you heard yet? We're rebranding the company and moving forward without your 10 Rules."

"Yes, I noticed in the last board meeting that they weren't included in your presentation, but I wasn't sure why."

Ironically, when I recruited Jim a year earlier to fill the role of Vice President of Sales, he told me that one of the key decisions for joining our team was our 10 Rules.

"I'll be honest with you Lloyd," he hesitated, and I could tell that the next words were hard for him, "they became a point of frustration for the team because it was clear they didn't apply to everyone equally. Rather than being an example for employees, the rules showed the hypocrisy of the, um, Senior Leadership."

I knew what "Senior Leadership" meant. He was talking about me.

After a pause, I admitted, "You're right, Jim, I can think of several examples where I acted hypocritically. But what about Rule 5? Vigorous Debate? Why didn't you speak up if you felt that way?"

"Are you serious? We did. Multiple times."

Those words hit me like a punch in the gut. He continued.

"It became clear that anytime someone was critical of an operation or employee, or a strategy, you or one of the other founding partners killed the debate. We decided it'd be better to just go along to get along. The 10 Rules only work if the leaders follow them too."

Ouch.

Brené Brown defines vulnerability as exposure, uncertainty, and emotional risk. The Vigorous Debate rule can be extremely difficult to practice, especially for a CEO who is a "know it all," like I was, complete with a roster of Sacred Cows who could not be challenged.

True vigorous debate requires that the CEO become vulnerable, exposing your ideas, leadership style, personnel, and organization to the uncertainty of what a team member might think. We naturally want to defend ourselves, our team, and our company when criticism occurs, even when that criticism is valid. To instead lean into the criticism and have an open and honest discussion about it, takes intention and discipline.

I really sucked at this, and honestly, I never mastered it. We excelled at vigorously debating the small stuff while avoiding the hard discussions about things that really mattered. My insecurity and refusal to be vulnerable in the way that Brené Brown defines cost me my team, and my role in leading the company.

Process–The Role of the CEO

The CEO should not be a participant in the Vigorous Debate process. Rather, their role should be limited to serving as the umpire, so to speak. Training the team in the skill of seeking to understand before seeking to be understood.

As a facilitator, the CEO brings topics to the debate process as well as curates topics from issues brought up by the team.

In the *Seven Habits of Highly Effective People*, the practice of seeking to understand, then to be understood (which we talked about in The Zig Rule) best describes the overall goal of the Vigorous Debate Rule.

The first part of the process is to form a question around the specific thing to be debated. The person that brings the question, item, or thing to the debate, should present in the form of a question.

Questioning

The foundation of seeking to understand is asking clarifying questions and listening with an open mind. As the umpire, a CEO's duty is to help everybody understand the rules of the game and let a team member know when they've gone out-of-bounds i.e., attacking a person's character rather than challenging their viewpoint.

The questions are not meant to be dismissive, but rather to remove ambiguity and establish clarity around the person's feelings and beliefs. Questions that are accusatory in nature should be avoided, at all costs. These types of questions are good in a courtroom but in a vigorous debate often put people in a defensive posture, which shuts down open dialogue and erodes trust.

When questioning is done well, the individual expressing their feelings or beliefs will feel heard, even if others disagree with them in the end. Most people don't mind if you disagree, but don't appreciate being told their thinking is flawed or not worth considering.

Listening

Active listening is hard, but it is a vital component of Vigorous Debate. This takes training and discipline, and should be practiced every day. Human beings are emotional creatures and maintaining objectivity when someone is discussing you, your team, or something you're invested in is extremely hard. The key is to listen for the complete narrative without allowing oneself to become defensive and angry.

One question that had, of course, surfaced during multiple meetings was what to do about Jay Miller. Jay violated Rule 3, the Golden Rule, with great regularity. We talked about him in chapter two.

Instead of practicing active listening to understand the root issue, I always shut it down. Jay was a Sacred Cow and I refused to listen and address the issue properly. Often when the debate was killed, it was because it was argued to the point where people just gave up and said "you're right" rather than sticking it out for a true resolution. "You're right" is a white flag statement, usually indicating a Golden Rule Violation (people feel as if they aren't being treated with respect). That's a failure and everyone loses.

Remember, the goal is to understand "why" they hold a particular view in the first place, not determine who's correct. Resolution comes later.

Reflecting

Here is a perfect example of holding the mirror for your team, as we discussed in the previous chapter.

Ideally, after going through the Vigorous Debate process, the issue at hand has been clarified for all parties involved and the reasons behind each party's stance have been openly explored. Often, when this is done well, the next steps are clear and everyone agrees on a course of action that is best for the team.

When there are two divergent paths forward, and both have their merits, the CEO has to make the decision on which path is best for the team or company. I have found most of the time, if the umpiring has been done effectively, having to make a judgement is rare. When these steps are followed, the members of the team feel heard and respected. The team will move forward with clarity.

Trusting

If people understand the rationale behind what's been decided, they can still support the initiative even if they would have made a different choice. Everyone may not be happy or agree with a judgment call, but everyone will feel as if they have been heard and understood, and that builds trust.

When a team has trust, there are very few limitations on the success the team can attain. When an organization really wants to be its best, to hit its Mark, the Vigorous Debate Rule will continually raise that Mark. The company will become strong, healthy, full of energy: vigorous!

A CEO that practices vulnerability creates a culture of trust. Steven MR Covey, author of *The Speed of Trust,* says that trust is the one thing that is common to every individual, relationship, team, family, organization, nation, economy, and civilization throughout the world—one thing which, if removed, will destroy the most powerful government, the most successful business, the most thriving economy, the most influential leadership, the greatest friendship, the deepest love.

When the team lost trust in me, they lost the trust that they could "go there" on any issue. It slowed down our company and we became unhealthy. The children's book, *The Emperor's New Clothes* is a story that best illustrates what happens when a leader lets his ego create a culture of total incompetence.

Teams that shoot for excellence in Vigorous Debate end up having a high level of trust, which leads to better communication, productivity, and overall team morale. With that, they can move fast and have a more realistic view of the performance of the company.

That's when the company starts winning more often, as measured by new customers, higher revenue, higher profits, and the ability to learn from their losses. As with sports, fun happens. The real job of umpiring is making vigorous debate rewarding for both the individual and the team.

What's the Point?

Engaging in the vigorous debate process is a healthy, uncomfortable exercise for any organization. It allows your employees to be heard, your leadership team to learn and grow, and the whole team to come together for an intentional, open-minded discussion.

TAKEAWAY
It's not about *who* is right, but *what* is right!

PROFIT FIRST RULE

THE CORE FOUR

For the organization to survive and thrive,
these four core rules serve as the foundation:

The Trust Rule
The Golden Rule
The Safety Rule
Profit First

Profit First Creates a Long-Term Environment for Fun

Companies are living, breathing organizations made up of people, products, and processes. The products and services that you provide in the marketplace must have the ability to provide a profit margin. This allows the business to scale and will provide stability for the growth. Understanding the relationship between cash flow and profit is important for a business in the same way understanding the relationship between calories and macros is for a competitive bodybuilder.

Compound Investment

Companies need to be fit, just like a bodybuilder performing at the highest level. Profit over time builds resources for a company to invest in growth, which usually means investing in people and assets like computers, vehicles, offices, manufacturing, and other miscellaneous things.

Looking back, I realize that one of the things I did not properly value was the time invested by our stakeholders to reach profitability and properly protect that investment. You invest more time at work than you do anywhere else. Time is your *most* valuable asset, as we discussed in The Best Rule.

In our largest revenue year, 2018, over 200 employees contributed more than 577,000 hours of labor. Focusing on profit first respects the resources invested by employees, equity partners, and customers. As a company grows, each of these groups have made an investment in your company. All of them have aligned with your mission and purpose.

Think about this, equity partners provided cash and credit to get the company started. The customer invested trust in your product or service and paid you. Employees invested their most precious resource, time, in your company to help it provide the products and services. Acknowledging the total investment of all stakeholders is WHY profit first is so very important. When reviewing or developing business plans, the first question to ask is, "Are we respecting all our stakeholders' investments?"

How can you understand the compound investment of all of your stakeholders? When you recognize the totality of an investment, you can accurately assess what strategies result in actual profit. For example, let's look at a very impressive year, 2010, on paper.

In 2010, our revenue grew by 875%, leading to a net profit increase of 2600% over the previous year. We grew from 15 employees to 51, and they collectively invested over 173,000 hours of work to generate this seemingly resounding return to profitability. However, what you don't see is the incremental investments made in 2008 and 2009 that made this growth possible. When you include the total cost of goods sold, salaries and wages, and operational costs from all three years, more than $11M was invested to generate a net profit of $2.6M.

Recognizing the real investment puts that one-year return in perspective.

Opportunities

It's fun to make money. (Profit is ALWAYS fun)

The media, the general public, and even employees, are often critical of companies making large profits. They fail to realize all of the benefits of profitable companies—they hire more employees, pay higher salaries and benefits, invest in more assets, and return dividends to their shareholders. Those shareholders usually invest those returns in other companies, their families, or important causes.

Today, many companies, after they've been consistently profitable, choose to support charities that mean something to the business or the owners—with many making investments in green technologies and giving to social causes. All of these investments are merely allocations of profit that directly benefit people. They are able to do this because they make enough to meet all of the needs of the company and still have remaining profit to share with others.

By acknowledging the total investment, Profit First is all about people!

> This rule was originally called the Fun rule, but as you'll see, putting the focus on fun can lead to poor decisions.

Balance

(Fun is not always profitable)

Wanting to have an environment that is enjoyable (fun) is understandable. However, if we focus too much on having a good time, we can—in the long term—create an environment that is worried about positive feelings for a moment versus long-term enjoyment.

In the fall of 2014, we started negotiations to acquire a company based in Houston, Texas. This company treated industrial water streams outside of the oil and gas industry. This seemed like the perfect opportunity to expand the company and move into a new market, and the acquisition company was greatly undervalued, in our opinion.

It was all very exciting, and negotiating to buy a business is honestly a lot of fun. We all got wrapped up in the promise of a huge return and what that would mean for our company.

The mistake was focusing on revenue diversification and growth without understanding the real value proposition and how that would be profitable.

During the diligence process, it became apparent that the company had many more issues. There were red flags everywhere: accounting errors, unidentifiable inventory, and lawsuits and other legal issues. In our zeal, we ignored the dangers and instead focused on negotiating a lower purchase price. We continued to focus on the fact that we were getting a deal, ignoring all the indicators to the contrary.

Our focus was on the fun of negotiation of an acquisition rather than the hard work of putting profits first, and it ended up hurting our company at every level, including having to lay off seven team members. Ultimately, the greatest cost wasn't the financial or productivity loss, but the loss of trust with all our stakeholders.

What's the Point?

Putting profit first is putting people first.

Focusing on the fun stuff is about feeding egos and recklessly attempting to meet board expectations. Fun became about pleasure and instant gratification. It's unhealthy for the business.

On the other hand, doing the hard stuff first can lead to more fun over time. Think about working out; I've been doing a CrossFit type program for almost 10 years, and there are days that it is not enjoyable, but the results always are. Likewise, when we take the time to focus on the hard stuff up front, the company is profitable, and we get to Celebrate (Rule 9)!

TAKEAWAY
Fun is not always profitable, but being
consistently profitable is always fun.

THE GOLDEN RULE

"Did you just call me a . . . man whore?"

Ted, one of our seasoned salespeople, stared at Josh in disbelief.

"Oh come on, don't be such a little baby about it," Josh laughed boisterously at his own joke, not realizing everyone else in the room was shifting uncomfortably in their seats. "I mean, would you have had dinner with Mr. Albertson if I wasn't paying you to be there? What's the difference? I mean if you think about it, I'm really insulting myself. What kind of pimp would keep you on board?" He laughed again and looked to his captive audience as if expecting an applause.

I wanted to disappear into a hole. Dreading a fight, I didn't want to engage Josh in front of the team. I felt like a failure, ashamed I didn't confront him. In reality it would have been good to engage in Vigorous Debate in front of the team because it would have solidified boundaries and shown courage and conviction in upholding Rule 3.

Josh had used that phrase with me in private, but I never dreamed he'd say something like that in public, let alone a team meeting. Some of the men laughed, most uncomfortable, but I could tell it really offended Ted.

"Josh" I said, as everyone began to file out of the room. "Stay behind for a minute, would you?"

"Sure, what's up?" He was in high spirits, obviously buoyed by his performance.

"You can't be saying stuff like that man. Calling the salespeople 'man whores'? You have to know how extremely unprofessional and offensive that is."

"Hey, I said that to you just yesterday and you thought it was funny! You need to chill out, it's from Deuce Bigalow, man. Everybody loves that movie."

"First, that was a private conversation between friends. A business meeting is a completely different environment. Two, it wasn't funny yesterday either, it just didn't seem worth the fight."

"Sure, sure… I get it." Josh said with a knowing wink, clearly missing the severity of the issue.

I sighed, "Just please keep your audience in mind for the future, okay?"

He stared at me for a moment, puzzled, before turning around and leaving without a word. I had hoped that would be the end of it.

It wasn't.

In fact, during one of our reverse performance reviews (we called them 360 Reviews) in 2019, it came out that he was still using the term. If anything, the issue got worse and became common language every time he interacted with the sales team. Almost every team member was bothered by it; however, Josh was one of my Sacred Cows, so no one had challenged him directly.

These performance reviews are generally anonymous, but the reviewer is given the choice to sign their name if they'd like. The term offended people so much that three members of my staff felt strongly enough to include their names on their reviews. Ted was one of them.

Josh has been a blessing to me in so many ways, but sometimes he has a low emotional IQ, not realizing the impact words can have on people. The ability to put himself in their place or see it through their eyes is not one of his strengths.

Josh is a strong personality and he fed on that laughter, which was why he continued using the phrase.

Seeds planted in that first conversation with me were watered with laughter during the meeting. I applied a single spray of weed killer after that first meeting, but didn't continue, and the seeds grew. As Josh interacted with the technical sales team, he used 'man whore' consistently. It became permitted, normal.

Since no one on the executive team called him out, including myself, the implication was that we endorsed the behavior. I'd had more than one conversation with Josh since the review about how he was hurting others, but Josh always blew me off, and I let him.

I guess I didn't want to have the conversation either.

It wasn't until the 2019 reviews that I understood the full extent of my own violation of the Golden Rule in that situation. It was the first time I'd been rated poorly, but I already knew I deserved it.

Farming for Success

Growing a company is a lot like growing a crop. There's a lot of preparation to be done before you even put your seeds in the ground, then you have to plant the seeds, then there's the long process of adding water and nutrients to the soil to nurture the plants. This is called tending the field and must be done intentionally and routinely to ensure the seeds we are planting reach their maximum potential at harvest.

In business, you have to tend to your organization with the same intentionality and consistency that the farmer brings to their field. Everyday you're developing relationships, setting guidelines, rules, standards, and best practices, all with the intention of maximizing the quantity and the quality of your business.

As I look back, I can see all the seeds that were planted that allowed our company to grow. We had unbelievable success in a relatively short amount of time. But I also allowed other seeds—weeds—to be planted in the company, whether through a lack of follow-through, allowing bad attitudes, or failing to hold myself and others accountable to commitments.

Bad Seeds

Even highly producing fields can still have patches of neglect. If you don't constantly ask the question "Are we treating others as they should be treated?" you may allow bad seeds to take root. If you allow weeds to grow deep roots, it's almost impossible to kill them.

The weeds can even take over the whole field. Remember: you're always feeding one or the other. Trust, or distrust.

With every interaction, you're planting, feeding, or growing seeds of trust or distrust. Treating people poorly, or by allowing them to be treated poorly by others creates an environment where weeds thrive. Those weeds of distrust use up nutrients, causing good plants to be smaller. The time and effort it takes to kill the weeds makes growing a healthy crop very difficult, and sometimes you lose the crop.

Not tending to the weeds can have very real consequences for you as a leader, as you unknowingly undermine your own authority.

Something I learned is that if you find yourself complaining about the actions of another person, you are sowing seeds of distrust. Complaining is like a tumbleweed for a company. When you as the leader complain, it becomes permissible for everyone in the organization. The tumbleweed starts rolling through the organization, depositing seeds everywhere.

Such was the case with a board member, original investor, and friend of mine, Doug. We had many conversations over the years, but towards the end we found ourselves disagreeing more often than not. We didn't honor the Vigorous Debate rule and instead complained to other board members, and embarrassingly, employees as well.

This lack of open communication allowed each of us to assume the worst of each other. For me, I assumed he had a lack of trust in my leadership. Rather than talking with him directly to confirm or confront this assumption, I allowed the seeds to take root, to grow out of control.

———————— ⌒ ————————

"Doug did it again," I exclaimed.

"What?" Jim, our CFO, asked.

"He's going behind my back directly to Bruce and telling him that the board wants to shut down the Mid-Continent District."

Bruce was the president of our logistics company, Smart Logistics, and had just recently been promoted to Chief Operating Officer.

"What??" Jim said with a combination of frustration and disappointment.

For the last couple of years, Doug had started arranging private meetings with the management team and causing confusion, sowing seeds of doubt. I had tried to address it before in one-on-one conversations with Doug. He would downplay these meetings, and sometimes deny he had even talked to a team member at all.

Bruce, in his new role as COO, had not been exposed to Doug and took everything he said at face value. This allowed Doug to subtly put a plan in motion to dismantle my authority as CEO.

Doug contacted Bruce, Jim, and the rest of the board, stating I was looking to delegate my responsibilities to Bruce. Then doing a quick phone poll, convinced the board to approve his suggested role changes.

The next day I received a call from our in-house attorney Mack, who was also a member of the BOD, confirming that my role had been changed. Going forward, all decisions about the company's operations would now be made by Bruce exclusively.

Doug had managed to remove my authority from my own company, *without me even knowing it*. Of course, I assumed the board was doing this intentionally out of a lack of confidence in me and I responded accordingly. I would not have my role as CEO diminished and if they wanted Doug and Bruce to run the company, then they would get their wish.

I contacted Jim and Mack to let them know that I would be resigning, effective the coming Monday morning. This conversation caught them off guard, since they believed that I had agreed to these changes. We had some very direct conversations, and all of us realized that Doug had manipulated this event and that we needed to have a board meeting immediately to resolve the issue.

This event was the final straw for many of our owners and investors. They no longer trusted the management team (mainly me) to lead the company and that's when it was ultimately decided that we should pursue selling the business.

Weed Killer

The best way to start killing weeds in your fields is to stop complaining. Next, go directly to the person that you were complaining about and start a conversation, using the skill of "seek to understand, then to be understood." This robs the weeds of a vital source of nutrients. Direct conversation starves the weeds and when consistently practiced, removes the nutrients for the weeds and eliminates the seeds of distrust, preventing them from being replanted.

As we move into the final two rules, keep in mind, how you treat others is a reflection of your trustworthiness. If you don't treat others right, they'll never feel secure and won't develop trust in your relationship. Treating others poorly ruins your credibility. Without that credibility, your people can't trust you.

What's the Point?

The Golden Rule is defined as treating others with respect, the same respect you would want to receive from them. This has less to do with how you expect others to act towards you, and more about how you expect yourself to act towards them.

Respect involves having hard conversations when something isn't right. If you want to encourage others to practice the Golden Rule, you have to consistently model it yourself first. Neglecting to address violations of the Golden rule, even temporarily, always results in planting, fertilizing, and growing bad seed into crops.

The health of your organization starts with you.

TAKEAWAY

People never forget how you treat them.

THE SAFETY RULE

If you don't go home at night,
no other rules matter.

It was a beautiful warm morning, July 16, 1984, and like most days I was operating a large front-end loader.

"Brown!"

I heard my boss yelling my name over the engine noise as he ran toward me.

"What's up, Bud?"

"Got a call from your mom, she needs you to head over there."

"Oh ok, I'll finish this last section and let you know when I'm leaving."

"Turn off the engine, Brown. You need to go home, now."

Dad.

Suddenly, a memory from the night before filled my mind . . . "Love you Pops, I'll see you tomorrow . . ."

That memory kept repeating in my head as I ran to the truck to leave.

I can't explain what I felt as I drove home. Sometimes I'll encounter something, and I feel as if I've lived it before—deja vu. Several times I had dreamed that my dad had died and at that moment, I was overcome with the sense that dream had become reality. *Please dear God, don't let it be Dad, please, oh God please!* As I rounded the corner to my parents' house, my driveway came into view and I saw several cars, including two police cars and my uncle Jimmy's.

My pastor at the time, Dick Clemmer, met me at the door. I could see my mother sitting at the kitchen table, her face in her hands, weeping. His face made it clear that it was more than just a bad feeling I'd had. Something was horribly wrong.

"Lloyd, I'm so sorry." He paused for a moment, breaking eye contact, clearly trying to collect himself. As he looked back up at me and began to speak again, I could see his lips moving, but it was as if I was in a daze, unable to comprehend what he was saying.

"Wait . . . what are you saying? I don't understand."

"Your dad, he was killed in a car accident this morning."

My mom ran to me, clinging to me in total despair.

I couldn't even bring myself to comfort her, I was so stunned by the news. Pastor Clemmer put his arm around my mom and gently led her to the couch. As the shock gave way to intense grief, I was so overwhelmed that I punched a brick wall. I'm amazed I didn't break my hand.

> It's not until you experience one of those moments that you really grasp the impact of one person's life and death.

———— ⌣ ————

The number of people affected by my dad's death was enormous.

In our family alone, my mom, my four sisters, aunts, uncles, and cousins, as well as my grandmother—my dad's mother—all directly shared in the loss of my dad. His death reached far beyond just our own family, though. As a business leader, community leader, and philanthropist, my dad's impact on the community was significant, but I didn't fully realize how many people he touched until his funeral. The day is forever etched in my memory.

As we approached the beautiful sanctuary of the First United Methodist Church, I couldn't help but remember how just three months before, we had held the grand opening. As the fundraising coordinator for the new sanctuary, my dad had been in his element organizing people around a cause.

It was a surreal moment to see a casket covered in red roses, holding his broken body, in a place where he'd been so alive such a short time ago.

Looking at the front row, I saw my own loss multiplied in the faces of my family. When I looked back at the overflowing sanctuary full of grieving community members, some of whom I had never even met, I was overwhelmed by the outpouring of love for my dad. In total, over four hundred people were in attendance at his funeral.

As we made our way to the cemetery, we drove past lines of firefighters, policemen, and oilfield employees. Each one having turned the lights on their hats off in respect. Through my grief, I couldn't help but feel pride at the positive impact my dad had on everyone he interacted with.

It had been raining that morning and was very dark and overcast, but when we arrived at the cemetery and got out of our cars, the sun suddenly broke through the clouds and shone down on us. It seemed as if that was the only bright spot in the world at that moment.

I've spent my whole life being the beneficiary of the oil and gas industry. It's been a blessing for my family—providing work for me and so many other people that I love. That said, it is a very high-risk industry.

When we made our 10 Rules, the Safety Rule had originally been rule number one. In the oil and gas industry, companies are required to have safety protocols, practices, and documentation in place just to be able to work. Insurance in the oil and gas industry is a significant expense because of its inherent risk factors.

I understood the exposure—previously, I was a risk manager working in the insurance industry helping oil and gas companies manage that inherent risk. When the management team set out to build our 10 Rules, the first thing that we all agreed had to be included was the Safety Rule.

Risk

Definition, **Risk**: *a situation involving exposure to danger.*

In business, there are three main types of risk: financial, physical, and emotional. The safety rule needs to address all of these risks to be effective.

As I discussed in chapter four with the Profit First rule, truly managing financial risk means having a very detailed process on how and when to make decisions to grow the company.

Too many times we only focus on the potential for positive financial impact, but we don't consider what may happen if the investment fails.

> Often it's tempting to focus only on the pot of gold at the end of the rainbow. We tend to forget that many rainbows exist in the eye of a storm.

CEOs must recognize that when they take a risk, it can put the company in jeopardy. Business is risky, however, and when a CEO goes all in, they must take into account the worst-case possibility, even while striving for the best outcome.

Engagement

Early one morning in late August 2015, my phone rang.

Early morning calls are rarely good news, so I was already anticipating the worst when Jay Miller, our safety director, informed me that one of our crews had an accident on their way to a job site.

As bad as it was to get the call, I was relieved to learn no one was killed.

As Jay recounted what happened, it was clear this could have been much worse. Our driver fell asleep at the wheel en route to the job site that morning. Miraculously, he woke up just before the collision, barely swerving away in time to avoid a head-on collision.

Had he not woken up when he did, he would have driven into the oncoming tractor trailer, likely killing everyone on board. Thankfully, instead, there were only two damaged trucks and one employee with a broken leg at the local hospital.

I was immediately transported back to my dad's funeral, thinking about all the people in attendance. Quickly doing the math in my head I realized that our crew of four, plus the driver, could have easily represented *almost two thousand lives impacted by their deaths.*

As more details emerged about the situation, we learned that his coworkers knew he was tired. In fact, they'd left him at the bar the night before to watch the Cowboys preseason game as they went back to corporate housing. The manager didn't insist he come back with the rest of the team and he ended up only getting three hours of sleep before taking the wheel.

I started asking Jay a million questions.

"Why didn't the manager bring him back with them?"

"Why did they let him drive, knowing he was out too late?"

"Why did he feel he had to drive, even when it was unsafe?"

It was a chain of bad decisions that almost cost five people their lives. All because my driver felt he needed to drive while exhausted to fulfill his duties, and *none of his teammates felt empowered to stop him even when their own safety was clearly at stake.*

At that moment, I realized that I hadn't been fully committed to creating a safe work environment for all stakeholders.

Lean Into the Problem

When there is a tragedy, a leader needs to run toward it, not away from it, so I immediately started looking at ways to protect our employees working in this area.

The crew involved in the wreck had been on their way to a remote job site in the Permian Basin, the largest oil- and gas-producing region in the world[1] and by far our busiest region. We had more employees in this area than anywhere else.

It also holds the distinction of being one of the deadliest areas to travel in, accounting for 11 percent of Texas traffic fatalities—as

[1]https://www.energyindepth.org/the-permian-basin-is-now-the-highest-producing-oilfield-in-the-world/

well as 43,661 vehicle crashes and 1,457 injuries in 2017 alone. Given the danger of this area, even those who didn't work for me directly could be affected by our safety practices—or lack thereof.

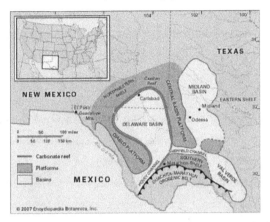

We recognized the most dangerous part of the day was driving to and from work locations and because of this, we wanted to provide a tool that would not only benefit our employees on the job but one that would impact their personal lives as well. After looking at various options, we ultimately invested in the world's leading crash-avoidance training program, the Smith System.

In addition to the new training, I also realized that we needed to be invested in each other as people first before we could ever hope to function effectively as a team. I wanted to make sure I knew every employee, and make sure they knew me.

> Smith5Keys™ is a process to provide drivers with the knowledge and skills to create three important tools for safe driving: Space to Maneuver, Visibility to Detect Danger, and Time to React. The Smith5Keys™ are: Aim High in Steering; Get the Big Picture; Keep Your Eyes Moving; Leave Yourself an Out; Make Sure They See You.

Starting Strong

Since the day of the accident, I've attended every new employee orientation in person, or I've called in. This is something that has given me great satisfaction. Not only did I get to know the employees, I made sure to ask about their family members and those important in their lives. I reciprocated by introducing myself and telling them about my family and why the Safety Rule was important to me.

This accomplished two goals: first, it showed the employee that we were invested in them, and that we understood that their family is an integral part of their lives; secondly, it allowed our new employees to instantly begin to see themselves in each other.

New Employee Orientation was also a time for me to set high expectations for safety based on a foundation of mutual respect and care. During this conversation we would review each of the 10 Rules, their importance, and how we practice them in the company. The Safety Rule was so important that it was the only rule that would lead to an automatic termination if intentionally violated.

It was during one of these orientations where I met a young man named Xavier.

"What division are you going to work for?"

"I'll be working in the water group, sir."

"Oh, that's great, it's a very important division. What will you be doing there?"

He looked at me timidly and said, "Sir, I've never worked in our industry before, so I'll be the low man on the totem pole."

I chuckled a little and asked, "What do you mean by 'low man'?"

"Well, I'm new, and like I said, this is my first job in the industry, so I'm starting at the bottom as an entry-level water tech. I just look at dials and walk around to make sure there aren't any leaks. Anybody can do this."

He was obviously deflated. He seemed to feel as if he was of low value simply due to his age and lack of experience. I vividly remember looking into his eyes as I said, "Your role is important to this company, or we wouldn't have hired you. We don't have 'low men' here. Plus, your lack of experience isn't a negative at all, it's a positive. It means that you have fresh eyes. You'll be able to identify things in our company that we may not see, since we've been here for so long."

I went on to encourage him to ask lots of questions:

What are we doing?

Why are we doing it this way?

Why is it important to our customers?

Have you ever thought about this?

I wanted him to be inquisitive. I let him know that on several occasions when a new employee has asked a question, it helped us improve our process, and there were several times the improvement of that process was key to the safety of our team and our customers.

"What are your goals?"

He looked confused. "I hadn't really thought about it honestly. I just thought where I started is where I would stay."

I let him know this was just the beginning of his career, and that he had all the opportunity to move up in our company.

This conversation convicted me so much as to the importance of making sure people know their value. When they feel valued and important, they begin to make decisions and have expectations of themselves.

The Stop Card

One other important point we touched on during new employee orientation was using what is called a "Stop Card." The Stop Card is a laminated card that allows any employee, as a representative of the company, to stop *any* job at *any* point to address a safety concern **on my authority**.

Stop Work Authority

Stop any job or procedure you deem unsafe
for yourself or your fellow team members

STOP

You will NEVER be penalized for stopping an unsafe job.

"Stop Card" created by Joshua Kerievsky, https://medium
.com/@JoshuaKerievsky/stop-work-authority-d853f6a3c42d

The Stop Card has a process, and steps to follow. Once a process has been stopped for safety reasons, the supervisor on location makes sure everyone has clarity and determines if and when a hazard has been mitigated. That supervisor then makes the final decision whether or not to resume working.

It doesn't matter what team or company is working on a project, ANYONE can stop the job. No matter who your team or supervisor is, you're still a human, and we're all responsible for ensuring the safety of ourselves and those we work with as we practice the Golden Rule.

Giving your team the authority to stop work no matter the cost takes courage from you, the leader, and it empowers your front-line workers. If they have to wait to ask permission, it can be too late, and lives and property can be affected forever. My team members knew that I would back them completely if they stopped a job for safety, *even if they were wrong*. That's true empowerment.

What's the Point?

While my Dad's death may have been one of the most impactful, it is far from the only loved one I've had to say goodbye to. I recognize that we're all going to die, but that doesn't mean we should be careless with our lives—doubly so with the lives of others.

Just as we must demand physical safety from all of our employees, we must practice financial safety in decision-making that could lead to layoffs, or worse. Just like with my dad, we don't know how many people any one individual may affect. As a leader, you can't just consider how the safety of your employees will affect your company, but how their death or injury would impact all the people who rely on them as well.

Knowing your people helps you truly understand the consequences of your decisions. That kind of understanding is a double-edged sword. You get the blessing of knowing when you have made a positive impact on someone's life, but you also have to live with the burden of guilt when you've had a detrimental impact. Making non-emotional decisions, in my opinion, is a way to avoid knowing the impact of your decisions. And avoiding the consequences of your decision hurts you, your team, and your organization. It's not just about business, it's about people.

TAKEAWAY

The Safety Rule completely encompasses the Golden
Rule by respecting the value of a human life.

THE TRUST RULE

Give Trust Earn Trust (Steven M.R. Covey)

"God? Are you there?"

The pistol feels heavy in my shaking hand.

It's the evening of March 18, 1993.

I'm sitting in our closet, alone, surrounded by an empty house, a brand new one we had just moved into and now just a shell of a home built on lies. It feels like a tomb.

"I'm such a failure." I said this as much to God and the barren clothing racks of my wife's dream closet, as I did to myself.

Why? I couldn't help replaying in my head all of the times that I had demeaned, insulted, belittled, and mistreated my wife.

My wife was out of town much of the time as a flight attendant, and I thought I enjoyed living like an unmarried man. Still angry about the death of my dad, I was escaping any way I knew how: strip clubs, bars, anything to make me forget. But I was living a lie.

Feelings of worthlessness overwhelmed me. I was at the lowest point in my life.

Only a week earlier, we had celebrated our sixth anniversary, and I'd just found out it would also be our last.

As I sat there thinking about ending the pain of failure, I prayed, "God if you are real and you love me, you need to show me."

I inspected the gun one more time, *this will be the one thing I am not going to fail at.*

Then, my phone rang . . .

Holly, my assistant, put the phone down, her sparkling eyes answering my question before I even asked it.

"Did we get him?"

"Confirmed!"

Stephen M.R. Covey, author of *The Speed of Trust*, had just agreed to be our keynote speaker in Smart Chemical's major marketing event in March, 2020.

Stephen's book had been vital to my growth as a leader, instructing me to build trust by first giving trust. We had been working on this event for three months, negotiating and establishing a contract with Stephen and hiring a professional company to help us stage and provide all the things needed to have a truly professional event.

In preparation for the event, we had multiple calls with Stephen and his team scripting out the evening and our speaking roles. Half of our annual marketing budget had been allocated to this event, and we'd been hoping it would be the catalyst to make 2020 a record year.

Our desire was to have a process to define an expectation of "Trust" that would break down the untrustworthy reputation the chemical industry had earned. This event centered around Stephen's book, and also the role it had in the creation of our 10

Rules. I was going to be working with the man who was instrumental in the development of who I was as a CEO. I felt a sudden sadness, as all I wanted at that moment was to be able to call my mom and tell her the good news.

None of this would have been possible without her.

———————— ⌒ ————————

"Hello?" I hoped my voice wasn't shaking as I answered the phone, the gun still in my hand.

"Are you okay, honey?"

"Mom?"

"I know it's late, but I had a terrible feeling and felt the Lord wanted me to check on you."

"I'm okay mom." *I think.* My heart was still racing from what I had almost done, and I was trying my best to sound as normal as possible, quietly trying to hide the gun, as if she could somehow see through the phone.

We talked for a while; I told her how empty the house was since Jamie left and she offered her support. My mom's feeling and intuition to call got me through that night.

The next day was a Friday and I had set my sales route, which was about a five-hour round-trip. A long time to spend alone with my thoughts. A time for shame to take hold. Realizing how often I had broken trust with my wife.

On the drive I thought about trust, and more specifically, how I hadn't been the best at earning the trust of those most important to me. I was able to recall countless examples of broken promises, missed opportunities, and untruths that I knowingly or otherwise, allowed into my closest relationships.

Looking back, I realized that I was often more deserving of trust with the strangers on the road, than my own family. When we drive our cars, we trust others on the road to follow the rules, and they trust us to do the same. When we eat at a restaurant, we trust that it has been prepared safely and won't make us sick, and they trust we'll pay for it at the end. These types of relationships are not normally personal. We trust complete strangers every day without questioning it, believing they will follow the rules.

Trust in interpersonal relationships is different. In *The Speed of Trust*, Stephen tells us to build trust by first giving trust. When we begin a new relationship, it's essential to give the other person implicit trust, the same way we do when we drive. Over time, if that trust is returned, a real relationship develops. This takes time and must be intentional; the key is you can't stop, you have to continue to trust.

Being alone with my thoughts on the road provided a lot of time for that reflection, and my thoughts turned to all the ways that I had failed in my marriage and broken her trust. This line of thinking snowballed into a regret for the countless other times I had broken someone's trust.

———————

> Originally the order of the rules was different from what you have read in this book. The trust rule was originally rule number three and followed the Safety Rule and the Golden Rule, but in reflection it became clear to me—all relationships must begin with the gift of trust and as such, undergirds the other rules.

The same need for trust applies to a company's relationship with their customers. The oil and gas industry, in particular, has a horrible reputation of being untrustworthy. Because of that, many people think of chemical companies as snake oil salesmen: "Whatever ails you we've got a chemical for that!"

I wanted to set a new expectation for the industry, one where Smart Chemical defined the expectation of "Trust" and that would break the well-deserved reputation that the chemical industry had earned.

We wanted our invitations to our March event to be unique in order to make an impact on those we invited. Brainstorming possible gift items took days as we considered and dismissed several different ideas.

"What about a small bottle of whiskey?" Holly knew that many of the invitees would be native Texans, and we love our whiskey.

"Whiskey, that could work." Personally, I had an interesting relationship with whiskey. It was attached to one of my darkest memories . . .

————— ⌒ —————

When I finally got home for the day after my long drive, I did my best to distract myself, pouring myself a glass of whiskey and sitting in front of the TV. I turned on the news but couldn't focus on the program.

My mind was stuck replaying all the mistakes that led to last night...*last night.*

My eyes instantly locked on the phone next to the chair. *Had it just been a coincidence?*

Ring. I thought to myself. *You made it ring last night, God. If that was real, do it again.*

Nothing. My mom wouldn't have any reason to call again, but I hoped anyway.

Ring! I screamed in my head.

The only thing I heard was the television commercial in the background. The sudden realization of being completely alone hit me with a forcefulness that physically hurt.

"Ring!" I said out loud, turning the television off and standing up. Now looking directly at the phone.

"Please ring." I whispered in a last-ditch plea.

Silence.

Moments later I'm back in my closet, with my gun, my mind racing, shame covering me like a heavy, suffocating blanket. Waiting...

I hold the cold steel in my hand, tempted by its promise to take all the pain away. No calls this time, nothing to stop me.

Not expecting an answer, I said a final prayer, just in case. "God if you are real and you love me, please show me . . . "

As we considered the whiskey idea, I just didn't feel like it communicated anything about trust, which was the main focus of our event.

"I want something that conveys trust, or direction, like finding your way through a dark forest with the help of someone you trust."

My staff understood that I was looking for something specific, but just couldn't visualize what item could convey the message I was trying to send.

I started thinking about foundations. The Cornerstone is the first stone set in the construction of a masonry foundation. All other stones will be set in reference to this stone, thus determining the position of the entire structure.

The foundation of the 10 Rules comes from the desire to provide all stakeholders with a definition and expectation of how we're going to work with each other. It also recognizes that the beginning of any relationship begins with giving trust. This comes from the definition of trust as being the firm belief and reliability of the truth, or the strength of someone or something, and the only way to have that kind of trust is to start by giving it, because it's not yet been earned.

> Rule 1, Give Trust, Earn Trust is the Cornerstone, or the beginning of building a strong relationship. Like a Cornerstone–Rule 1, Give Trust, Earn Trust–sets the expectation of our relationships and becomes the foundational reference point when there are challenges in any relationship.

Giving trust and earning trust must be an intentional decision. Looking back on the 10 Rules, each one of them set an expectation of how to do business and what personal responsibilities are expected of each individual as a member of our team.

When beginning a new relationship my first desire is to give trust. It's a personal expectation to give every individual the gift of trust. To do that, I found that I must identify any prejudice that I may have based on experiences with people that weren't positive, and realize that I may miss the gift of a great new friend if I'm not open to giving trust. Giving trust in the beginning of relationships gives the greatest opportunity for blessing.

I've come to realize that trust in relationships is like constructing a building brick by brick, stone by stone, instead of pouring one gigantic slab of concrete and tilting the wall up all at one time. If there's any flaws within that tilt-up wall it's going to crumble, but if you build it brick by brick, while it may feel like it's slower, you end up with something much more solid. If one brick has been misplaced, it's usually easier to repair than tearing down the whole wall and starting all over.

Each moment in a relationship is like one of those bricks. Every interaction we have is us placing another brick in the wall and sometimes it feels like certain bricks were placed there by God himself.

The doorbell, followed by a loud banging on my front door shook me back into reality, and I nearly dropped the gun in surprise.

After getting myself together and hiding my gun I opened the door to find one of my best childhood friends waiting.

"Ben?" My shock and disbelief must have shown on my face. I honestly couldn't believe he was standing there.

"Hey man how are you doing?" Ben looked at me, concern in his eyes, "Everything ok? You look like you've seen a ghost."

"No, just surprised to see you. Are you lost?"

"I was on my way home to Lubbock . . . been in Albuquerque the last few days. I decided to go the long way and come see you. You know me man, 'I live my life by a compass, not a clock.'"

My puzzled expression led him to explain.

"It's a quote by this guy in a book I just read, his name is Stephen. . . . Stephen Covey, I liked it."

"True north! A compass! What if we order a nice compass for each invitee and engrave it with the Smart Chemical logo, and call the event Find Your True North?" I exclaimed as the memory washed over me in a moment.

My team agreed that a compass would be a great vehicle for the invitation, and Holly set out to find the perfect compass that wouldn't use up the whole budget.

Now that we had the name of the event along with the central piece for the custom invitations, we personally delivered the invitations to the key people from companies that we wanted to attend. In this invitation, we included the beautiful brass compass in a wood display box with the Smart Chemical logo inside, and announced that Stephen Covey would be our speaker.

The results spoke for themselves; the event was a resounding success! Our customers that attended publicly validated that we were a company that was trustworthy. Those who were not already customers approached me and other team members saying they were looking forward to doing business with us because they felt like we truly understood their concerns. My new partners, my two founding partners, and the other members of the team were congratulating each other for resetting the bar and celebrating what these new relationships would mean for our company.

Our team did such an amazing job of coordinating the aspects of this event, especially my executive assistant Holly Artho. I can say that in the 13 years I spent leading this company, the preparation for this event and the collaborative effort of our team was the closest we'd ever come to really hitting the mark. It was so close to perfect.

I really don't remember a lot of the rest of my conversation with Ben, but I remember my conversation with myself later that evening.

Lloyd you have to make a decision, are you going to believe the evidence that God answered your prayers, or do you believe that the answered prayer both times was just a coincidence? It's time to make a decision!

Two times, two days in a row, I asked the same question and got the same answer through two of my closest relationships. I gave God trust by asking the question, and he earned my trust with his actions. That evening I called the senior pastor at my church, Jim Smith, and he agreed to meet me at 7:30 Saturday morning.

The next morning, I shared with him my experiences over the past two days and how God had proven himself to me. I told him, "I gave God trust and he came through, twice. Now I'm ready to give Him my trust every day for the rest of my life and give my life to Jesus." We talked for a bit after; Jim was very generous with his time, making sure I fully understood the commitment I was making. I said, "YES, I am intentionally giving my trust, my faith in God, through his son."

What's the Point?

Trust is the Cornerstone, the beginning of building a strong relationship. Like a Cornerstone—Rule 1, Give Trust, Earn Trust—sets the expectation of our relationships and becomes the foundational reference point when there are challenges in any relationship. Thus, trust undergirds every interaction we have in business and personal relationships.

TAKEAWAY
To change lives, you must intentionally give trust.

WALK TO EMMAUS

The Rest of the Story

As Paul Harvey would say, I would be remiss if I didn't share with you another story of trust returned.

In late June 1994, I attended a weekend retreat called "Walk to Emmaus." This retreat began on a Thursday evening and ran through Sunday, and was meant to serve as a time to learn about the many ways that God has given, and continues to give us, his grace.

During this weekend I met a gentleman named Paul, who had attended a previous walk and was there to support first-timers like myself. I shared with him that my wife, Jamie, and I were still in very turbulent times trying to rebuild our marriage, about how we had been attending counseling, and that she had just recently moved back home on a trial basis. Paul listened intently and compassionately, before sharing his own experience.

A year earlier when Paul attended the walk to Emmaus, he was also dealing with a troubled marriage and returned home to discover his wife had left him. As shocking and painful as the experience was, he recounted the blessings that he had experienced in the years since. He continued to encourage me over the weekend and the last night, he invited several others to join him in praying with me. Continually he confirmed his trust in God.

That Sunday evening as I returned home, I noticed that all the lights were off and the house was empty.

Jamie had left again, for good this time.

Strange as it may seem, I was suddenly overcome with an overwhelming sense of peace. Because of my experience with God's grace that weekend, I knew I could trust that everything was going to be okay.

On the walk that weekend, I had told God, "I know you are real and you love me, and you have showed me. I TRUST YOU." And that trust was what got me through that event, and all the others you've read about here, and it's the same trust that motivated me to share these lessons with you at all.

When it came time to write this book, as I mentioned in the introduction, my intention was to go through how each rule could benefit you as a leader. However, as I started with The Learning Rule and went back to examine the lessons I had learned, I realized my own failure to live up to the standards set by the 10 Rules is where the real lessons were learned.

That was a tough pill to swallow and I had to deal with my shame, and I had to choose to get better not bitter. Following Rule 1, Give Trust, Earn Trust, I am trusting God by admitting these failures so you can learn from me. My hope is that you can see the failures for what they are, moments of regret, not the sum total of me. In the same way, when you fall short of your ideal self, remember not to internalize those feelings like I did.

However, when looking back at all the wonderful people I have had the pleasure of working with and all the incredible things we've done, I see the truth. I needed to go through the failure to prepare me for the next step in my journey. Every day was a mixture of success and failure, both large and small. The important thing is to not be complacent with success nor dwell on failure, but remember who you are and that your journey isn't over.

TAKEAWAY

Failure is an event, not who you are!

When you get burned through the fires of life, by giving trust to God, he will use it to refine you!

ACKNOWLEDGMENTS

I want to first thank my wife Lora, who has always believed in, and expected, the best of me. She always reaffirmed her love for me even when she was getting burned by the fires of my failure.

To my daughter Bailey, for always believing her dad is the best even though I haven't always deserved it.

To Steve Brown, my advisor, who always challenges me with new ways to look at the world, and who planted the seed that I should write a book.

Thank you James and April, my writing team, for always asking questions that required me to clarify this message. You both encouraged me to trust the reader with my intimate failures to help them avoid, if possible, some of the painful lessons I have learned.

To my best friend Kurt, my Barnabas, for standing beside and behind me, and leading me when I struggled with courage or energy to move ahead.

To my strategic coach Mike Marchi, a great friend, who always asks the hard question: "why."

To my mental coach, Twilla Woolsey, for helping me break unhealthy thought habits though understanding why they started and how they undermine my relationships. Thank you for teaching me the training methods for my mind to be healthy and strong.

To the authors whose books inspired me to set the boundaries that helped me move forward and accelerate, and who I refer to many times in this book: Andy Andrews, Stephen M.R. Covey, Stephen R. Covey, Brené Brown, and Dave Hollis.

ABOUT THE AUTHOR

C. Lloyd Brown is the cofounder of Smart Chemical Services, L.P. and currently serves as Vice Chairman of the Board. Additionally, Lloyd founded the consulting practice, www.RefinedbyFailure.com. He serves on the Amarillo Economic Development Corp and is the former Chairman of the Board. Currently, he provides mentoring services to the West Texas A&M Enterprise Center as the Entrepreneur in Residence. He is a serial entrepreneur and is an active owner of several other businesses. Lloyd resides in Amarillo Texas with his wife Lora and daughter Bailey.

CPSIA information can be obtained
at www.ICGtesting.com
Printed in the USA
BVHW030613150521
607367BV00005B/887

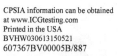